"The question is not what you look at, but what you see."

Henry David Thoreau

A BETTER LIFE

GOAL SETTING, VISUALIZATION

&

THE LAW OF ATTRACTION

Robert Lawrence, ATP

Contact information:

vegetarianpilot@gmail.com

Twitter: @RobLawrence1966

Robert Lawrence at Facebook.com

Dedicated to the memory of Wayne Dyer, PhD.

Thank you for sharing your wisdom with the world.

Contents

INTRODUCTION

"You are not stuck where you are unless you decide to be."

Wayne Dyer

You are able to create a better life. Whether you believe it or not, you are deserving and worthy of improved health, higher income, and more joy in your life.

For most of us, the biggest obstacles to creating a better life are our unconscious beliefs. They quietly keep us trapped inside our "comfort zone" and prevent us from achieving the lives we only dream about, but never truly believe possible. In this book, I explain how I changed my unconscious beliefs, enlarged my comfort zone, and overcame a life of mediocrity. More importantly, I share how you can do the same. I wrote this book because I am passionate about self awareness and human potential, and I know my suggestions will work for you, just as they have worked for me. I also wrote this book to prove that I can become an author using the principles discussed in this book. Not just an author, but a successful author. If I cannot manifest my goal of becoming a successful author, then you shouldn't believe anything I write. After all, in this book I expect to convince you that you can create a better life by simply changing how you think and visualizing your outcomes. I have used the same techniques to move from the rain to the sunshine, graduate from a respected university, find love, inner peace, happiness, and economic security. I was even able to manifest a career as an airline pilot at age 49!

I am writing for those of you who are ready to try something new because what you have been doing has not been working. You probably hear the nagging voice inside your head telling you that you're deserving of so much more in life, and you are. I caution that you will need to have an open mind to accept what I am sharing. While the ideas are not new, they might be new to you. As a young man, I knew I was capable of more in life, but I didn't know how to get out of my rut. I didn't like my job; I was broke; I had several bad habits; and I was totally unfulfilled. Fortunately, I had an experience which allowed me to begin seeing life differently. I came to understand that my subconscious thinking had kept me tethered to mediocrity. When I finally understood that my thinking had been holding me back, I changed what I thought about and my life began to improve.

I could probably explain how to improve your life in just one or two pages; however, since most of us believe that change is difficult, I am obliged to write 17,000 words to convince you that what I am saying is true. Your thoughts are powerful and creative; what you think about expands.

Have you ever listened to a person talk about a goal they wanted to achieve, but immediately after stating their desire, the person expressed several reasons why they could not accomplish their goal? This is why people stay stuck in life. Our conscious mind declares one thing and our unconscious mind proclaims the opposite. We have all been guilty of this self-defeating behavior. However, our past does not have to create our future. Our current thoughts create our future. If you keep thinking the same limiting thoughts, then your future will be identical to your past.

During the past two decades, I have focused on what I want in life instead of focusing on what I don't want. I currently live in a beautiful home located on a golf course with views of the sea; I have a partnership in a sailboat; I have travelled the world, and I am fit and healthy and I share my life with a loving wife and several rescue cats. I even left an unfulfilling career and became an airline pilot at age 49. Most importantly, I am happy. I share this information not to boast, but to persuade you that you can also achieve a better life.

When I ponder the meaning of life, I always arrive at the same conclusion. I believe humanity and everything in existence is connected. I believe there is "some-thing" which has always existed and this something is without beginning and without end.   It has no boundaries. This something must be infinite. I call it "Source." Others might call it God, but I prefer to say Source because the word God has become synonymous with religion. Religion brings comfort to many, but it also divides people, and I choose to not take sides.

Source is the creator of everything. Therefore, humanity must be created from Source. We are expressions of Source and therefore, we are also creators. Everything we create begins with our thoughts. Our thoughts and emotions are our direct connection to Source.

If you're a fan of self awareness and spirituality you are probably familiar with the work of Dr. Wayne Dyer. I wrote two letters to Dyer before he passed in 2015, thanking him for the wisdom he had shared in his books. Along my journey I have listened to thousands of hours of podcasts and lectures from Esther Hicks, Bob Proctor, Earl Nightingale, Louise Hay, Deepak

Chopra, Napoleon Hill, Alan Watts, Tony Robbins, and countless others. These icons have shared their messages of self-empowerment because it was their passion. They had no choice but to share. Following in their footsteps, I decided to become an author myself because I share the same passion. What began as a thought is now manifesting as a book, right before my eyes.

In this book, I will share how I was raised, and what I was taught to believe. I discuss how my unconscious beliefs shaped my life and kept me in a rut until my late 20s. Mind you, the rut existed only in my mind, but as you know, our minds control our bodies and determine our outcomes much like a hypnotist controls a willing subject. I once saw a stage hypnotist convince a volunteer that he was a chicken. The volunteer, a friend of mine, began strutting and clucking on stage after hearing a trigger word. My friend was completely believable and later confided that he felt as if he had been in a dream, and he didn't understand why he had been clucking like a chicken. I know why. Because his subconscious mind had temporarily accepted that he was a chicken; therefore, he acted outwardly as he believed inwardly. We all do.

If your subconscious mind believes that you are a failure you will behave accordingly. Your subconscious will deliver whatever it has been programmed to believe. Your subconscious is powerful. It can outwardly manifest confidence and success, or it can manifest a chicken. To illustrate, think of a farmer planting two crops in his field. He plants one row of poison ivy, and in another row he plants corn. The earth returns exactly what was planted. The soil will not grow roses where poison ivy was planted. The earth does not judge. Our subconscious also delivers whatever we plant. If we plant doubt and fear and sickness, our subconscious mind has no choice but to return fear and sickness and doubt. If we plant thoughts of fearlessness, perfect health and certainty, our minds will return certainty and health and fearlessness. It is a law, similar to other laws found throughout nature. What is your subconscious telling you? Just look at your results in life and you'll know!

In a prior job, before I manifested my career as a pilot, I was fortunate to work with people who often struggled with substance abuse, poverty, or mental illness, among other things. My employment during that time allowed me to share words of support and encouragement to people who had often lost the support of their friends and family. On occasion, the recipients of my support reported back to me years later, to share how they had improved their lives. I recognized that a simple word of encouragement had emboldened others to obtain their GED, enroll in college, get sober, or pursue their passion.

Words of encouragement cost nothing, but everybody benefits. That's why I always suggest that you offer sincere compliments generously since they are free to give and can make a person feel better immediately. If you share a big smile and say "thank you" to a cashier, they might share your kindness with the next customer, and your kindness will create a chain of events, which may result in several people feeling better, all because you thanked a person for their service. The opposite is also true. If a person is rude to a waiter, the waiter might feel hurt and be unkind to the dishwasher. Then, the dishwasher might feel offended and share their hurt with a family member later in the day. I don't want to be responsible for hurting innocent strangers, so I always try to be kind. Words are powerful.

Over the past two decades, I have shared my ideas with friends and others who have expressed an interest improving their lives. Sadly, however, most people have no curiosity in self-empowerment. It is a rare individual who can break free of "group think" and chart their own path in this world. The idea that a person can create the life of their dreams is too foreign for most to comprehend, let alone accept. Too many of us are preoccupied with driving the right car and following the latest trends that we never stop to imagine what's important and possible for us. Fortunately, I have never been concerned with the latest trends or felt a need for expensive cars or trinkets. I'm not trying to keep up with reality television stars; I don't care what brand of shoes I wear; and I'm not embarrassed if my wife's handbag is not sold on Rodeo Drive in Beverly

Hills. I believe that spending money in order to impress people only enriches others, while making the spender poorer. Also, people will never become fulfilled by acquiring more stuff, especially if they're just buying more of what they don't need.

I cherish new experiences over new possessions. I prefer to sail in the open ocean, meet new people, travel, and perform improv or standup comedy. It's important for me to get out of my comfort zone. I like the personal challenge of participating in a marathon or triathlon or an arduous hike in the mountains. Mostly, I enjoy walking on the beach near my home. All of these activities are either free or affordable. I learned long ago that saving money would allow me to retire young, providing more time to do what is important to me. This is not a financial book, but I suggest you think about your financial future, for unless you die young, time will pass and the only thing worse than getting older is being both old and broke. I suggest you read a book by Joe Dominguez, titled, "Your Money or Your Life." After reading his book more than two decades ago, I changed the way I spent and saved. Small changes over time resulted in huge outcomes. In this book, I write about manifesting more money in your life, but I caution you that it's not always about how much you earn; it's also how much you save.

PART I

HOW WE CREATE OUR LIVES

"The subconscious mind cannot tell the difference between what's real and what's imagined."

Bob Proctor

We create our lives with our thoughts, both consciously and unconsciously. Our thoughts are often just endless chatter in our heads. One moment we might be thinking about the weather, and the next moment we are wondering why the traffic is slow. Our random thoughts are interrupted only when we need to focus on a particular topic. When we focus our thoughts we become powerful. When I focus a ray of sunlight with a magnifying glass, I can ignite a fire.

Focusing a camera lens can bring clarity to a distant image. When we focus our minds, we are capable of greatness. Without focus, we drift aimlessly.

Our thoughts are non-physical energy, and they manifest in our brains as electric signals. But the greatest minds do not agree where our thoughts originate before they reveal themselves in our brains. I believe that all thought emanates from infinite Source. Where else would a thought come from? In fact, I believe we all share one infinite mind. That's why we connect with each other, and how we can sense what another person is feeling.

CONSCIOUS VS. SUBCONSCIOUS

"Whatever we plant in our subconscious mind and nourish with repetition and emotion will one day become a reality."

Napoleon Hill

Thoughts are directly related to consciousness, but what is consciousness? According to the infamous psychoanalyst Sigmund Freud, the conscious mind includes everything that we are aware of, including our memory. For example, while seated before my computer I am using my conscious mind to craft words onto the screen. I think about word placement and sentence structure using my conscious mind. My conscious mind is my point of awareness in this moment.

The subconscious or unconscious mind is more puzzling than the conscious mind because it lies beyond our everyday awareness. In *The Power of Your Subconscious Mind,* Joseph Murphy wrote, "You must make certain to give your subconscious only suggestions which heal, bless, elevate, and inspire you in all your ways. Remember that your subconscious mind cannot take a joke. It takes you at your word. "

Our subconscious represents our mental programming, our software and our core beliefs. Our subconscious receives all information from our conscious mind, regardless if the information is true or false. Our subconscious then acts on this information. For example, if you tell yourself that you have a bad memory, your subconscious mind will insure you're forgetful. If you think to yourself that everything is too expensive, your subconscious will insure you never have enough money. If you frequently think that you are overweight, your subconscious will insure you never get thin. Your thoughts create images in your mind, and your subconscious delivers the image to you as reality. Your unconscious mind does this without emotion or judgment, just as planet earth returns whatever was planted by the farmer. We reap what we sow.

Some people believe consciousness is a function of brain activity. However, I have often heard the human brain described as an "electrical switching station," much like a computer, collecting and distributing data according to algorithms written in software. An algorithm is simply a formula for solving a problem or completing a task. If you input the same information in a computer, the computer will always return the same results. It has no choice.

In addition to creating computer software, humans also created computer hardware. Hardware is the external casing and circuitry inside a computer. Software and hardware must join together for a computer to come alive. Human consciousness operates similarly. Our physical bodies represent the hardware and our consciousness mind is the software. We need both our body and our mind working together to have a human experience. Our subconscious mind brings our body to life. My subconscious does not argue. It believes what my conscious mind instructs it to believe. Everything we think, hear, and accept as true imprints on our subconscious. Our programming determines how much money we are comfortable earning, and how confident we feel in any situation. Humans do not behave randomly; we behave according to our internal programming, just like a computer. Remember when your computer science instructor said, "Garbage in, garbage out"? Our programming determines how we live our lives! Our internal dialogue emanates from the programming we received as children, and the programming continues throughout our lives.

Every belief you hold emanates from your subconscious mind. If you were taught that money makes people greedy, and you believe that greed is bad, your subconscious will keep you poor in order to protect you from becoming greedy. Your subconscious does not judge, just as a computer algorithm does not judge. Until we change our programming, we will continue to obtain the same results we have always gotten. This is why people earning $25,000 yearly at one job will usually earn $25,000 at their next job. They subconsciously believe their time is only worth $25,000 annually. This is also why diets don't work long term. People continue to see themselves as they have been; instead of seeing themselves as how they want to be. The picture you hold in your mind is always your outcome. Change your picture and you will change your outcome.

Before I became aware of the power of my subconscious mind, I sought work that paid only a slightly higher wage than I had earned at prior jobs. For example, if I was earning $10 hourly at my current job, I would not consider applying for a job paying $20 hourly because my unconscious mind did not "believe" I was deserving of the significantly higher wage. I falsely believed that other people were more qualified and deserving of higher incomes. My unconscious beliefs held me captive within my comfort zone.

Fortunately, you can rewrite your personal software and change your life. You can change your life for the better or for the worse. It is entirely up to you. This is how it works, whether you believe it or not. The same force that beats our hearts and rotates planet earth insures that everything manifested begins with a thought. This is true for every person, not just you. We are not separate from Source; we are expressions of it. We are creators. Accept this and understand that you create your life with your thoughts. You can attract more wealth, more love, more happiness, and even the body you imagine by changing how you think and what you 'believe' you can achieve.

This talk of reprogramming our minds seems simple enough. However, overcoming years of limiting and negative programming can be difficult, especially if we didn't write our initial program and aren't even sure how a computer works. I'm not saying that it is easy, and it's unlikely to happen overnight. At age 50, I'm still overcoming the negative programming I received in my youth. Some of my programming is buried deep, and it is fighting to hold on. This is why I continue to surround myself with like-minded people and repeatedly listen to inspirational recordings and read self-improvement books.

To begin improving our lives, we have to begin sending appropriate information to our subconscious mind. You might resist my suggestion because you were taught to reject anything you consider too good to be true. Is it too good to be true that earth provides oxygen for us to breathe and water for us to drink and food for us to eat? Is it too good to be true that the sun provides our planet with unlimited energy? Source provides everything. However, we take this natural abundance for granted because we are born into it. The magnificence of Source is hidden in plain sight.

POWER OF THOUGHT

"Thoughts become things. If you see it in your mind, you will hold it in your hand."

Bob Proctor

Most of us are familiar with the term "placebo."A placebo is generally thought of as a pill containing no medication. We have heard stories of patients who are prescribed a sugar pill but are told by their doctor that the pill is actually a new, revolutionary medicine, which has been proven to cure a particular ill. When told of the power of this amazing new medicine, the patient often "cures" their ailment after taking the miracle pill, despite the fact that the medicine was merely encapsulated sugar. Since the pill contained no medicine we must conclude that the patient's mind provided the cure.

Placebos can also be mental suggestions. For example, in her 1998 New York Times article, Sandra Blakeslee cites a study of arthroscopic knee surgeries, in which some patients received only tiny incisions in their knee, but they reported the same amount of relief as patients that underwent actual surgery. This study and other placebo studies have exposed the power of our minds. Our bodies know how to heal, usually without any intervention. My body is magnificent, but it can only lift a couple of hundred pounds. However, my mind can figure out ways to lift thousands of pounds, and more. My imagination has no boundaries except what I give it. The thoughts I think repeatedly become my beliefs and my beliefs shape my outcomes.

I am sure we all know a person who tells themselves and others that they will get sick every winter because it is cold and flu season. And they do get sick. Some people actually believe walking in the rain without an umbrella will make them sick. If they get sick, it's because their mind manifested the illness. If rain made a person sick, then taking a shower would kill them. This is an example of a false belief and the power of the mind. The same also holds true for those who believe walking outside in freezing temperatures will make them susceptible to catching a cold. This is ridiculous. If this superstition was true, then Canadians would be sick all the time and Hawaiians would never be sick. Personally, I believe I am immune from everything and I see myself as healthy and fit. And I usually am.

PART II

AN AWARENESS

"In the infinity of life where I am, all is perfect, whole and complete. I no longer choose to believe in old limitations and lack. I now choose to begin to see myself as the Universe sees me – perfect, whole, and complete."

Louise Hay

The experience I am about to share really happened and it underpins the entire book, so I am going to disclose a very personal of story. During my mid and late 20s I lived in Seattle. I was a hard worker, but I was generally unhappy and was aware that I was not living up to my potential. But something happened one day that forever changed my life. I was alone in my apartment when I had an out of body experience. Not a near death experience, but something more appropriately described as awareness, or an awakening. I wish I could paint a brilliant picture for you, but I have no recollection of seeing a golden light or interacting with spiritual beings. Perhaps I did, but the memories were erased. It was not a vision, it was an understanding. It was a knowing.

During the out of body experience I became aware of our true nature. I understood that human beings are part of a greater, infinite collective. Others might use the word "God" but I choose to say Source as my experience was not religious. It was spiritual. While sitting at a table, unexpectedly, the invisible veil separating human existence from Source parted and for the first time in this life, I became aware of our infinite existence. I remembered that we are all connected and there is nothing to fear.

I use the word veil because I now understand that there is an invisible, penetrable barrier which conceals infinite Source. The veil surrounds us at all times but we cannot see it. Just because you have not yet experienced this veil does not mean it doesn't exist. It exists just as air exists all around you, although you cannot see the air.

If I only had one word to describe Source, I would choose the word "love."I am not saying that Source is love. The emotion associated with Source is similar to the emotion of love, magnified times infinity. When I passed through the veil and (re)connected with Source, I understood that death is an illusion and fear is a wasted emotion because there is no beginning and no end to Source. I became aware that we are infinite Source, currently expressed in physical bodies. I understood that with Source there is only now. Memories of the past and thoughts of the future are always experienced in the present moment. I understood that time is a mental construct, which was created by humans to make sense of this reality. Like Deepak Chopra says, "Now never ends."

The answer to every question was understood. Everything I needed to know, I knew. The veil of my human existence had been lifted, and I was one with Source. It was pure ecstasy. When I crossed back through the veil, and returned to my human existence, memories of the event quickly faded, like water running through my fingers. I grabbed a pen so that I could record the experience. But it was already too late. I retained the greater understanding but not the details.

Following the experience, I remained in a state of bliss and was unable to sleep for the next two nights as energy was pulsing through my body. I was desperate to understand what had happened. I even attended religious services for several weeks in an attempt to make sense of the event.

Attempting to describe the experience is like trying to describe a color to a person who was born without sight. A color cannot be explained. How can you describe the color red to someone who has never seen a color? A color must be experienced. To fully comprehend Source it has to be experienced also.

Following the awareness, I began reading books by Wayne Dyer, Louise Hay, Deepak Chopra, Alan Watts and others in an attempt to make sense of what had occurred. The experience was too big for me to understand at that time. However, I learned that others had shared identical encounters, and they, too, had struggled to find the right words. I understood that I was not alone and what had happened was real. It had been a life-altering gift. My awareness had expanded.

Years later, in a moment of inspiration, I understood that consciousness exists separate from our bodies because my body did not pass through the veil, only my consciousness, my awareness, the eternal me. Our consciousness is the gateway to Source. In consciousness we feel, express, and experience Source. I now understand what is meant when others say, "We are not souls in a body. We are bodies in a soul. "Soul is another word for consciousness, and consciousness is another word for Source. We are consciousness. Our bodies allow us to have tactile experiences. Our bodies have an expiration date, our consciousness is timeless. When we die we cross through the veil and reunite with Source, and we remember everything. We come into human form for the adventure, to pass time in infinity, to feel with hands, see with eyes, hear with ears, taste with tongues, and smell with noses. We come here for adventure. But we forget we can never die, so we stress and worry while we are here. We fear death because the unknown is terrifying to us. We feel alone and powerless here. But we keep coming back because the upside to humanity is amazing. We experience the birth of our children; we fall in love; we watch sunsets and sunrises, and we share intimate moments with friends. We laugh and we cry and we fight and we forgive. We care about each other and we miss each other when those we love are gone. This is life. There is nothing else like it. We feel emotions so powerful that tears flow from our eyes. We appreciate how good we have it when we see how awful life can be. Tragedy exists next to beauty. It's all jumbled together. It's a risk, but we take it. Because the love we feel, there is nothing else like it, except Source. But with Source there are no surprises. Everything is known. Everything is ok. But Source lacks adventure, that's why we keep coming back! So remember, there is nothing to fear. All your worry gets you nowhere. You end up exactly where you will.

Why I had my out of body experience, I don't know. Perhaps I had the experience so I could share it with you. I was not meditating. It was unexpected. But having it allowed me to understand that infinite Source beats our hearts and looks outward through our eyes. The power of Source is 'our' power. Source is literally everything. There is nothing it is not.

WHY?

"…You are part of a universal consciousness, and there are no accidents in it. In your true essence—not the false self, not the ego part of you, but in the true essence of who you are—you are infinite and you have something very profound to accomplish while you're here. Otherwise, you wouldn't be here."

Wayne Dyer

In the twenty plus years since my out of body experience, I have thought about it endlessly. I have never had a repeat experience, except during a period of meditation the veil parted ever so slightly, and I felt the warm glow of Source. I have come to believe that "something" cannot emerge from nothing. Therefore, there must be something which has always existed. This something is without beginning or end. Everything must be part of this something since there is nothing it is not.

Most of us were taught as children that God created us, but we were also taught that the creator is separate from us. We were told that the creator was either a god or maybe even an explosion in space. The ancient beliefs never rung true since there can be no separation from infinity. The scientific explanation also falls short since the big bang requires "something" to create the bang. These two theories are attempts to explain our existence. But in the end, the only explanation that has ever made sense is infinite Source. We are expressions of Source, therefore we are infinite. We were created and we are creators. We are infinite potential. Our nature is boundless.

Given that we are infinite Source, expressed in physical human form, what is the point of our existence? I can only conclude that Source knows everything that has always been and knows everything that will be. However, to know everything which is unknown, Source allowed part of itself to forget.

By incarnating and forgetting that we are infinite Source, we experience both the known and the unknown. We are infinite possibility in human form. We are non-physical Source manifested into physical bodies. Many of you will resist this idea because I am professing that everything is connected. If you were taught that we are separate from our creator then my suggestion may not agree with your beliefs, which may have been programmed into your subconscious mind when you were young and defenseless.

People originally rejected the teachings of Copernicus because nearly all humans living at that time had been told that the sun, stars, and planets orbited Earth. He discovered that Earth actually orbits our sun. Copernicus offered a revolutionary proposal because it went against commonly held beliefs. But remember, our beliefs do not determine what is true. Something is either true or it isn't. The truth is not a democracy.

When you look at the sea, you might think of a wave as separate and distinct from the ocean. But a wave is an expression of the ocean. When a wave crashes on a beach it does not cease to exist. The wave always returns to the ocean--its source. People are like waves. We see ourselves as individuals and some believe that when we die our existence is over. But the reality is that we are expressions of infinite Source and when we die we return to Source because there is nowhere else to go.

If you look at any part of your body under a powerful microscope, you will see that you are a collection of atoms. We are comprised of protons, neutrons, and electrons. With magnification we understand that on the atomic and subatomic level we are in constant motion. We are generally unaware of this motion because it is happening below our awareness. Humans are mostly empty space, yet we are also comprised of trillions of cells, which themselves are miniature universes. We are energy in motion. When a person has a heart attack and dies, the dead body is "shocked" with energy in an attempt to return it to life. Energy is our life force. Energy is Source.

After our physical bodies die, the atoms continue their never ending movement and eventually form new molecules, circulating throughout the biosphere as other elements or energy. Scientists have proven that energy cannot be destroyed. Energy only changes form. For example, a match contains energy. When I strike a match the energy contained in the match becomes heat and light. The energy can never disappear because it is a byproduct of Source. Since Source is everything there is nowhere for the energy to escape.

<u>OPPOSITES</u>

"The word happiness would lose its meaning if it were not balanced by sadness."

Carl Jung

Everything has an opposite, except Source. Infinity has no opposite since there is nothing opposed to infinity.

For us to know positive, we must know negative; short is required to know tall, hot to know cold, life to know death, fast to know slow, cruel to know kind, known to know unknown, and so on. If everything has an opposite, then the opposite of physical must be non-physical. We are physical beings created from non-physical Source.

Source must be consciousness since there is nothing Source is not. Source must be everything we can think of and everything that we have yet to think of. We are not created from no-thing; we are created from Source. Similarly, non-physical thought is required to manifest every physical human creation. To illustrate, an architect must first think about designing and building a house. After she has the original thought, the architect designs the home with her thoughts and oversees its construction. The house began with her thought. Thoughts are formless energy, which can create a house or a car or a space ship. Without non-physical thought there would be no human creation. Non-physical thought is consciousness. Just because we cannot see consciousness does not mean it does not exist. Likewise, certain sounds exist at frequencies outside our ability to hear them, but the sound waves exist nonetheless. There is much more happening than we can detect with our five senses.

In our modern world, there is invisible data moving through and around us via satellite transmissions and radio frequencies. This data represents nearly all knowledge available to humanity. We can capture this information via an internet connection; you can type any question into a search engine and receive an answer. The information is present at all times, but we cannot see it with our eyes. Source is also present at all times, but much of humanity is unaware of its presence. We connect with Source using our thoughts, emotions, and our subconscious mind. Emotions are universal and don't require translation from one culture to another.

PERFECTION

"We do not "come into" this world; we come out of it, as leaves from a tree."

Alan Watts

Everything is perfectly designed. We are passengers on spaceship earth, hurtling through an endless universe. Earth rotates about its axis with unwavering precision although there is no visible force applied to maintain this rotation. Earth's constant rotation distributes sunlight across the entire globe, effortlessly. We take our planet for granted because she asks nothing of us, but supports us just the same. It should be evident that the power which sustains earth is the same power beating your heart. That power is Source.

The oceans (there is only one ocean in reality) support life by creating breathable oxygen, nitrogen, and drinkable water. Moisture evaporates from the ocean and is lifted upward until it cools and condenses, finally becoming visible to our eyes. Clouds drift silently across the sky until the moisture falls as rain, collecting in valleys, rivers, and lakes. That's why we have mountains, so we can have valleys. Everything has an opposite. We must have mountains or the planet would be flat and there would be no lakes, oceans or rivers. It's all perfectly designed. We can place an apple seed in soil and Earth creates a tree. The tree creates fruit. It happens without our intervention. Earth is made of the universe and the universe is made of Source.

Source holds atoms together, rotates planets, digests food, and grows babies in their mothers' wombs. Despite the appearance of Source all around us, we go about our lives without considering the enormity of it all. We become distracted by the petty chatter in our minds and fail to see the wonder which surrounds and supports us. Because we dwell in Source, we are blind to it, much like sea creatures don't know the ocean exists because all a fish knows is the ocean. Fish only become aware of their environment after they are pulled from it by a hook or a net. The ocean surrounds and supports all life within it, but fish do not "see" the ocean unless they escape its grasp. Similarly, humans usually do not see Source because it is all we have even known.

When you mentally "step back" and think about the interconnectivity of everything, when you gaze at the stars in the night sky, you may understand that none of this is an accident. There is something greater than humanity, and whatever it is, we are part of it. We can tap into this something, our Source, and use its power to our advantage!

CONVINCED

"The universe sees itself through our eyes."

Deepak Chopra, MD

I am convinced that we are not meant to know all the answers while we are having our human experience. Knowing every answer to any question defeats the purpose of this adventure. As Source, we fully understand and accept that once we incarnate into human form, we agree to forget. After all, knowing the outcome of every situation would be no fun. If you knew every answer to any question asked on a television quiz show, you wouldn't bother to watch the program. If you won every hand of black jack or poker, you would quickly tire of playing card games. If you knew the outcome of every sporting event, you would never bother to watch another game. If you knew the ending to every story, you would never read another novel or watch another movie. We need mystery and contrast to make life interesting and exciting. We need a loser to know a winner. We need sadness to know happiness. We need defeat to know victory. We need death to know life. We need misery to know joy. We need dislike to know like.

We are not created to lead lives of suffering. Suffering exists because in order for us to have all possible outcomes, all outcomes must be available, including suffering. It does not mean that suffering must be our outcome 100% of the time. It simply means that suffering is an option. Life must include randomness to be exciting.

PART III

THE PROBLEM

"What we focus on expands."

Wayne Dyer

Many of us remain unfulfilled in life because we never learn that we alone are the creators of our lives. As I child, I did not learn about goal setting, the power of intention, or the law of attraction. When I refer to the law of attraction, I am suggesting that what you focus on expands. Like attracts like. A smile attracts happy people and a scowl attracts angry people. The image you visualize in your mind manifests as reality. We are constantly attracting people, places, things, and emotions because of the law of attraction. I call it a law because like gravity, the law of attraction works consistently, without judgment or emotion.

I don't recall my parents or teachers telling me that I am responsible for creating my life. Even today, my friends and family often do not appreciate the importance of goal setting, visualization, and positive affirmations. Not only do my friends not understand the law of attraction, they often do not care to understand. There are exceptions of course. Recently, I was speaking with a neighbor who is a very successful realtor and investor. I mentioned that my book is nearly finished and he asked about the topic. When I told him the book is about the law of attraction and the power of our mind, his eyes lit up and he responded that he has personally used the law of attraction to create his life and build his business. He told me that he visualizes outcomes in advance and he repeats a positive internal script to stay focused and insure success.

The power of Source is not hiding. Source is waiting for us. Our connection with Source is unbroken, but we first have to understand that Source is not just "out there," Source is also within us. Our connection to Source is our subconscious mind and our thoughts and emotions.

I suspect most people only talk about self improvement, never intending to change, because it is easier to repeat what we know than embark on a new and uncharted path. People fear changing their employment more than they fear spending 40 years of their life working at a job they do not enjoy. The good news is that negative programming, also known as scarcity thinking, can be replaced with a positive belief system. We just need to understand that we are creators and all things are possible. When we think a thought of fear or lack we must dismiss it, and replace it with a positive thought. We do this by keeping the bad news at bay and the small thinkers at a distance. Read books like this and listen to inspirational podcasts and attend self awareness seminars and bring friends into your life who encourage and support you. The fact that you are reading this book suggests that you are ready to accept total dominion over your life.

I do not blame our parents and others for our scarcity thinking. Our parents and others simply repeated to us what had been taught to them. Prior generations grew to become teachers and parents themselves, and they, in turn, shared their beliefs with their students and their children and the cycle of negative programming is repeated. While there are many notable exceptions, only in the past century have self improvement voices such as Napoleon Hill, Louise Hay, Earl Nightingale, Bob Proctor, Wayne Dyer, Esther Hicks and so many others offered a new and different way of thinking; a way of thinking which can significantly improve your life.

<u>WHY WE ARE UNAWARE</u>

"We seldom realize that our most private thoughts and emotions are not actually our own, for we think in terms of languages and images which we did not invent, but which were given to us by our society."

Alan Watts

Most of us acquire beliefs which mirror those of our immediate family or community. We soak up surrounding dogma because as children we were unable to protect ourselves from outside influences. To illustrate, consider how children acquire language skills without any effort. We learned to say "mah mah" and "dah dah" without knowing the alphabet or the difference between vowels and consonants. We learned to speak because we heard others speaking. Similarly, this is why it is normal to wear business suits and evening dresses in one society and burqas and flowing robes in another. In one society, it is normal to have canines as companions while another society may believe it is normal to eat dogs for lunch. One society eats cows and another worships them. People adopt the cultural norms and beliefs of their community. As a result, we unknowingly accept belief systems that do not serve us.

SCARCITY THINKING

"Few realize that they can control the way they feel and positively affect the things that come into their life experience by deliberately directing their thoughts."

Esther Hicks

Scarcity thinking is a belief system which suggests there is not enough of everything to go around. People who believe in scarcity imagine they are undeserving or incapable of attracting more wealth, health, and happiness. Our entire economic system is predicated on scarcity. The television tells us to "act now" as the sale is ending soon, and the supply is low. We value rare coins and baseball cards because there are "only a few remaining."We trade our labor to purchase rare gems and diamonds. But these items only have value because we collectively agree they have value. If I become stranded on a deserted island, my rare coins and brilliant diamonds become worthless. Real value is found in friendship and family and health and giving and achieving and so much more. Enjoy your trinkets but do not become obsessed with them.

In an infinite universe, there can be no scarcity. An infinite universe is without beginning and without end. Since everything which exists resides within an infinite universe, there cannot possibly be scarcity. It defies logic. Scarcity only exists in the minds of people who do not understand that we are expressions of infinite Source. Do not believe others when they speak of scarcity. Have empathy for them instead. If they ask, remind them that we are blessed with endless abundance. Human beings created money, so we can always create more. There can be no shortage of happiness and love since happiness and love are emotions, and we create emotions within our limitless minds.

PART IV

THE SOLUTION

"Every thought we think is creating our future."

Louise Hay

Once you accept that you can manifest your dreams using your mind, your life will change. In this moment, understand and accept that you alone are the creator of your life. Once you acknowledge your power, follow these steps and create your reality.

1. Decide what it is that you truly desire.

2. Write out your desire and display your written goal where you will see it often during the day.

3. Select a date when the goal will be completed.

4. Visualize your desire as if it has already been accomplished.

5. Feel the emotion of your completed desire.

6. Take inspired action.

DESIRES

"Set your mind on a definite goal and observe how quickly the world stands aside to let you pass."

Napoleon Hill

We are creators and the law of attraction is the delivery system for our desires. Choose your goal wisely. I only select one big desire or goal at a time. I look at my written goal throughout the day and read it aloud. When I do this, I'm using my senses of sight and hearing. The more senses you can involve the better.

I don't focus on goals because I believe they will increase my income or status. Status is a desire of the ego. My ego is like a container with a hole in the bottom and it constantly needs to be filled or it leaves me feeling empty. Ignore the ego, for it is always offended. As far as money, I am not overly concerned about money because I know that it flows to me naturally when I am receptive to wealth entering my life. Just as a tree delivers fruit without struggle, Source delivers abundance with ease. Expect abundance and it will come. Expect scarcity and it will come too. Your mind is a garden, and it returns what you planted with your thoughts. Plant wisely.

WRITE IT!

"Setting goals is the first step in turning the invisible into the visible."

Tony Robbins

Once I decide upon my goal, I either write it down on a 3 x 5 index card or type it on my computer and print out several copies. I place one copy on my desk, tape a copy on my bathroom mirror, keep one copy in my car, and place one copy in my wallet. That way I'm guaranteed to view my goal throughout the day. This is important because we have so much chatter in our minds that our desires will get lost and forgotten if we don't write them down. Studies have shown that ideas can be forgotten in 30 seconds or less, so capture them before they vanish!

VISUALIZATION & EMOTIONS

"Picture yourself in your mind's eye as having already achieved this goal. See yourself doing the things you'll be doing when you've reached your goal."

Earl Nightingale

I believe visualizing your goals and desires is the most important step in creation. Our minds see in pictures. Every thought you have is either an emotion, a voice in your head, or an image in your mind. You don't usually see words and letters scrolling across the theater in your mind. You imagine vivid memories or a vision of the future. These images can create powerful emotions. I often think of my dear cat Svarten, who returned to Source recently, and I see him in my mind and my heart aches because I miss him so much. I also think of all the wonderful memories of Svarten riding on my shoulders and a smile appears on my face. These memories appear in my mind as images, not as text.

If you desire to change your career, see yourself in your new career. Visualize yourself driving to the new building or location where you will be working. Visualize your workspace and your coworkers. See yourself enjoying lunch in the cafeteria. Imagine what you're wearing. Feel the emotions and hear yourself giving a presentation or chatting with your colleagues. Imagine yourself performing the work itself. If you see yourself as a nurse, see yourself in your uniform, tending to a patient. Hear the sounds that you will hear in your new environment. Think about your work schedule and congratulate your future self for having achieved your goal. Before becoming an airline pilot, I "saw" myself in my pilot uniform while greeting passengers as they boarded the airplane. I imagined my future into my never ending now, using my thoughts.

BE REALISTIC

"If you are not willing to risk the unusual, you will have to settle for the ordinary."

Jim Rohn

If your goal is to stay home and watch television the rest of your life then you can create that too, if that's what you truly desire. Perhaps you already have sufficient money to make that desire a reality. If not, maybe you will meet a person who will be willing to support you financially. You might find work as a television blogger and you can watch television and work from your computer while lying on the couch. Or, perhaps you will obtain employment editing television shows for a local broadcaster. I know of a young man whose only job is to watch videos and provide interesting videos clips to his employer. He actually gets paid to watch movies and television. One way or another your desire can become your reality.

Take note, you must believe that your goal is attainable. If you're 92 years old and 5' tall, your goal of becoming the leading scoring in the NBA is probably not something you really believe. I believe we must have faith in our goals or they are unlikely to manifest.

PART V

TAKING ACTION

"You are the master of your destiny. You can influence, direct and control your own environment. You can make your life what you want it to be."

Napoleon Hill

Once you have begun visualizing your written goal and feeling the emotions associated with your desire, you will begin receiving inspiration. When I'm focusing on a goal; I receive ideas and suggestions in my mind as to how I should proceed. When ideas appear in my mind, I record them in my phone. If I am inspired to write a letter or make a call, I make sure to do so as soon as possible. Source communicates through my subconscious mind so I take advantage of the inspiration and take action. The actions I take insure that I connect with the right people and allow my desire to gain momentum. Just like honey bees are required to pollinate a flower and rain is required to satiate a thirsty plant, all creation works in harmony. We are all connected. If you remain isolated you wither. This is why it is considered punishment to place an inmate in solitary confinement. We are connected beings, and we thrive when we work together.

I use the Internet to research my goals and learn what others have done. When I decided to become a pilot, I went to the airport. If I decided to become an attorney, I would go to a law school and imagine myself as a student there. I wouldn't worry about the expense. I would sit in a courtroom and watch the proceedings. I would begin taking action, any action, so that I could create momentum and allow the image in my mind to become more vivid.

When I decided to write this book, I configured a work space that was inviting. I began visualizing my book for sale in a book store. I created a cover for my book and wrapped it around a book I already owned, so it appeared as if my book already existed. Before I participated in my first triathlon, I watched YouTube videos to learn how to swim efficiently. I then I joined a gym with a lap pool. I just began taking action. Small steps led to bigger steps. We don't have to know every step before we begin. We just have to begin. If I decide to drive across the country, I don't have to plan every mile of the journey. I just have to begin driving and know that the route will unfold before me.

Because we all emanate from Source, and we are all connected, once we move in the direction of our desires, the law of attraction will begin placing the right people in our paths. You will meet others who are already doing what you want to do. You will learn how they did it. You may learn of a scholarship which will cover tuition. You may be offered an internship. You may even be fired from your current job. If so, see your firing as an opportunity. Steve Jobs, the co-founder of Apple Inc., said during a commencement speech at Stanford University, "You can't connect the dots looking forward; you can only connect them looking backwards. So you have to trust that the dots will somehow connect in your future. "He added, "Your work is going to fill a large part of your life, and the only way to be truly satisfied is to do what you believe is great work. And the only way to do great work is to love what you do…"

<u>BODY IMAGE</u>

"You have been criticizing yourself for years and it hasn't worked. Try approving of yourself and see what happens."

Louise Hay

Besides money, it seems that many people are displeased with their current weight. Fortunately, the law of attraction works for all things. The law of attraction uses the images we hold in our mind's eye and transforms our mental images into physical reality.

To achieve my desired body I always visualize the same image. I imagine myself with a professional swimmer's physique. I still eat pizza and ice cream and chocolate, but by visualizing my desired body image, I naturally eat healthy most of the time, and I gravitate toward exercise. I try to get to the gym three times weekly, if I'm able. I have weighed approximately 200 pounds for more than a decade and I feel healthy and I am fit. No diets, no rigid schedule. Just an image in my mind, and I allow the universe to work out the details. If you aren't sure what to do at the gym, you can hire a trainer or just observe somebody who has the body you want and imitate what they do. However, always check with your doctor before beginning any new exercise regime.

I don't beat myself up if I miss going to the gym for a few days or if I eat pizza three nights in a row. I know Source will insure I return to my path of health and fitness. It's as if I am on auto pilot. As a pilot I often have to adjust my heading to avoid other aircraft or weather. However, once clear of the threat I simply reengage the navigation function and the aircraft resumes its preprogrammed course. I don't worry about a temporary deviation while flying, just as I don't worry about temporary deviations from my eating and exercise habits. Surely the Source which created the universe can manifest the image I hold in my mind's eye. My body doesn't create my mind. My mind creates my body.

WEALTH

"What we think about ourselves becomes the truth for us."

Bob Proctor

Wealth, like anything, is also a state of mind. We generally expect to receive in the future what we got in the past. Ultimately, our income is based on our inner dialogue and the service we provide to others. The more service we provide, the greater our income. Working harder isn't always related to more income. If I work hard at digging holes, all I have at the end of the day are lots of holes.

Instead of just working hard, we should work at what we enjoy. By doing what we enjoy we are bound to provide more service and value to more people. If you're a salesperson who loves what you're selling, you'll serve more people. If you're a mechanic and you love what you're doing, you'll have more work than you can handle. If you're a barber and you love your work, people will line up to sit in your chair and when they do you can charge more. You can also hire people to do what you're doing and earn a percentage of what they're earning. If you are just working for a pay check, your employer will pay you just enough to keep you from quitting and working elsewhere.

Be open to receiving more money. See yourself as a money magnet. Money represents energy, so welcome the energy of money and it will be attracted to you.

<u>YOUR CHOICE</u>

"People with goals succeed because they know where they are going."

Earl Nightingale

Once we replace subconscious thoughts of doubt and scarcity with hope and passion, we can create the lives of our choosing. Just visualize what's important to you. I currently see myself in Maui writing my next book. I visualize walking on a beautiful beach, eating healthy foods, and body surfing in the warm ocean water at Kaanapali Beach. If fail to stay connected to positive thoughts, and instead spend hours watching television news and reading the local paper, I risk falling into my old thought patterns. Negative thoughts will attempt to convince me that Maui is too expensive; the world is dangerous and full of poverty and misery; the rich are greedy, and strangers are not to be trusted. But in my own experiences I know that people are generally kind and generous and good.

If I allow myself to believe in scarcity, my mind will try to convince me that I am foolish, my book will not become a best seller and nobody will want to hear me speak about the law of attraction. The negative part of me is alive and well. Negativity exists in all of us. However, I recognize negativity for what it is. Negativity exists so that we may know positivity. I understand that negativity is an option that I can choose. It is my choice.

Use the law of attraction to create more friendships or live where you want. Use the law of attraction to retire or change careers or enjoy your current career more. The law of attraction works with and for you. You cannot force it upon another because others have free will, just like you. You cannot change others, but you change how you think of others. Become aware of how you are thinking and then decide to think different thoughts if your old thoughts are not serving you. Your emotions will tell you if you are on the right path. If you are angry, then choose a different path. Make positive thoughts dominant in your life.

Do not be ruled by fear. Know that fear is a necessary emotion so that you may know fearlessness. Choose fearlessness. If you don't like something, know that you can choose the opposite. Don't blindly accept the opinions of others. Others are often living in fear and are unaware of the law of attraction. Don't be angry with those who hold thoughts of scarcity and negativity in their minds. Live your life as an example of how they too can live. Everybody will be ready in their own time.

PART VI

OVERCOMING OBSTACLES

"If you want to be successful, find someone who has achieved the results you want and copy what they do and you'll achieve the same results."

Tony Robbins

Nearly every day, I overhear people talking about their dreams and aspirations. These same people then immediately state all the reasons they cannot achieve their goals, or make changes in their lives. For example, I recently travelled on another airline and since there were no seats in the cabin, I sat in the flight deck. During the flight, the first officer spoke of his desire to purchase a home in Southern California. He then immediately said it was too expensive to buy a home where he wants to live. He talked himself out of his dream within seconds of proclaiming his desire. This is typical. I suggested to him, with his permission, that he should first decide what he wants and not worry about how he will achieve his goal. He just needed to know that he can own a home in the neighborhood where he is currently renting. After all, millions of people own real estate in Southern California. This pilot went on to tell me that he was earning $139 per flight hour. Given his income, he should have no problem purchasing a home anywhere in California. I have owned several homes simultaneously in Southern California when I was earning much less than this pilot. I focused on buying property instead of worrying about my income, and I allowed Source to take care of the details. In response, banks lent me money; responsible renters appeared; the mortgage was paid, and everything worked out.

When this pilot told himself that he could not afford to live where he desired, he eliminated the possibility of his goal becoming reality. If he had he written down his goal and visualized his new home, Source may have provided a single family home or a duplex, which would have allowed him to rent out an extra room or separate unit to offset the mortgage payment. He might have met someone who wanted out of their mortgage and needed a buyer to take over their existing payment. He missed the opportunity to have money arrive unexpectedly. There are untold ways he could have achieved his dream of buying a home, but he immediately fell into scarcity thinking. I am sure he did this unconsciously. Like so many others, this pilot was unaware that the obstacle to purchasing a home was his scarcity thinking, not his income.

During my travels, I also overhear people returning from vacation, telling other passengers how they dream of someday living in Hawaii or California or somewhere sunny and warm. However, these dreams require change; therefore, they are a threat to their comfort zones. To protect their comfort zones, these dreamers immediately remind themselves of all the reasons they cannot possibly make a change, just like the pilot mentioned before. This negative inner dialogue is due to the programming that often infects our subconscious minds. When threatened, our subconscious mind scares us into believing irrational fears, such as: "it's too expensive," "there are no good jobs," or "you won't know anybody."Our minds react this way because we have been bombarded with negative thoughts since our birth. We are told "no" hundreds of thousands of times as we grow into adulthood. We are surrounded by people who live in fear, and they share their fears freely with anyone within the sound of their voice. We are inundated with negative news from around the world via television, radio, newspapers, and the Internet. We hear stories of murder, and rape, arson, theft, disaster, and failure day after day. We have to search for success stories because the media focuses on fear, misery, and death. Remember what you're up against and be aware of your inner dialogue.

DISCIPLINE

*"If you really want to do something, you'll find a way.
If you don't, you'll find an excuse. "*

Jim Rohn

My main focus in life is being happy. I try to spend the majority of my day doing things that fill me with joy. If sitting at the computer for two hours would cause me misery, I take a day off. I listen to my emotions. If I dread going to a party, I don't go. If I am excited about going to the gym, I go. My emotions know what brings me pleasure so I listen to them. Source communicates via my emotions; therefore, when I'm feeling the emotion of love, I know I'm aligned with Source.

When sit down to work, I set a timer. I keep my phone out of reach and out of sight. I take breaks when the mood strikes and return to the computer when I'm ready. Like Esther Hicks says, "We will never get it all done."That's so true. I will never get everything done in this lifetime, so I remember that I am not in a race, and life is not a competition. I always have discipline when something is important to me. If I am lacking discipline, it must not be important.

PART VII

MY STORY

"Remember, it is not the thing believed in, but the belief in your own mind, which brings about the result."

Joseph Murphy

I grew up in Edmonds, Washington, a beautiful town nestled on the shores of Puget Sound, just north of Seattle. Looking back, I can see that as a child and young adult, I often heard scarcity statements such as: "We can't afford it," "Money doesn't grow on trees," "It is not possible," etc. In my immediate surroundings, nobody aimed high or thought big, and goal setting was never a topic of conversation. My parents were good providers, and they instilled a solid work ethic in all their children, but each of us kids also absorbed a belief that mediocrity was acceptable. That "good enough" and "getting by" met the standard for success.

I was cautioned that I should earn good grades in school, and when I finished high school I should find a job and work hard. I never learned to set and achieve goals, and the only thing I was taught about money was how to balance a check book. Balancing my check book was easy because I never had much money. Consequently, when I graduated high school, I found myself working in the shipping & receiving department at a retail store near my parents' home.

I was never passionate about working in a warehouse. I had taken the job because it was available. I had no plans to attend college because college was for successful people, and I was not destined to be successful because I had believed that I was just average. I had no plans to pursue my dreams because I don't recall that I had any dreams. Thus, I was like many young adults. I did not know what I wanted to do with my life, and my only plan was to eventually find a better paying job.

After several months of working in a warehouse, the nagging voce inside my head informed me that a change was needed. My solution was to enlist in the military. During the winter of 1985, I met with a recruiter and committed to serving 4 years in the army. I was stationed in Fort Benning, Georgia, for basic training and airborne school. I look back now with pride for having served in the military, and I certainly respect others who have served. In the Army, I did as I was told (most of the time), but I had no real passion for the work I did. I was a special operations soldier, which meant I jumped out of airplanes and descended to earth via parachute. Upon landing, I became an infantryman. Being an infantryman meant I was often cold, wet, tired, and hungry. I enjoyed the comradery and serving my country filled me with pride. However, the life of a soldier did little to quiet the nagging voice inside my head. No matter where I went--there I was.

After four years of military service, I returned to the civilian world in 1989. I moved back to Phoenix and found a job working in a different warehouse. On a positive note, I began attending community college with the help of educational benefits provided by the military. Two years later, I earned an Associate of Arts Degree. I had just turned 25 years old, but I was broke and living with my father again.

Feeling lost and unfulfilled, I again felt a need to "jump start" my life. That nagging voice inside my head just wouldn't go away, so I returned to Seattle and found a job working part-time in a bingo hall. About one year later, I obtained a better paying job with a well known snack food company. I was working six days weekly, 12 to 14 hours daily, and I was miserable. Although I was earning more money than I ever had before, I still lived paycheck to paycheck, and I had no long term plans. I had zero passion for the work I was doing, suffered from low self-esteem, and had only a few hundred dollars in the bank at any given time. I felt like a hamster on a wheel. I couldn't get off the wheel because I had to pay rent, car payments, and other expenses. I felt lucky just to have my job, although I hated going to work. I got out of bed in the morning and drove to work because I believed I had few options. I was frustrated and unfulfilled, and I didn't know how to change my life for the better. Like many people, I masked my unhappiness with bad habits. I did not eat healthy food, watched too much television, and did not exercise regularly. None of my bad habits moved me in a positive direction. The nagging voice inside my head was growing louder.

MY LIFE CHANGED

"Don't die with your music still in you."

Wayne Dyer

One day everything changed for me. As I mentioned earlier, I had an out of body experience in my twenties. In the weeks and months that followed, I began reading books in an attempt to understand what had happened. Fortunately, one of the books I read explained that most of us live our lives as if we are adrift in a rudderless boat, drifting wherever the current takes us. Most of us do not have any particular destination in mind so we never set a course, just hoping one day we will end up somewhere better. The author explained that in order to move forward in life, we simply need to decide what it is we want. By adding a rudder, we can point our life (boats) in a particular direction. By doing so, we will eventually reach a destination.

It seemed so obvious. I realized that I had been drifting aimlessly because I had never selected any particular destination for my life. I was reacting to life instead of creating it. I decided in that moment to select a goal and record it on paper. I kept the written goal in a location where I would see it throughout the day. It is very important to capture our goals by recording them. We have thousands of meaningless thoughts during the day, and our goals are bound to become lost in the chaos of our mind if we fail to commit them to paper or elsewhere. It is imperative that you record your desire and place it where you will see it or hear it throughout the day.

The goal I chose was to attend the University of Washington (UW) in Seattle and earn a bachelor's degree. Once I decided upon that goal, my mind immediately presented me with dozens of reasons why I might fail. That was how my mind responded at that time. Our minds remind us of all the things we were told by others--those who caution that it's too expensive, too hard, or takes too long, etc. But those who offer such advice merely repeat what had been told to them. They are mistaken.

Obstacles soon presented themselves. I went to the UW campus and discovered that not all of the college credits I had earned in Arizona several years earlier would be recognized, so I would have to earn additional credits before I could apply for admission. I was a military veteran, and I already possessed a two-year college degree, but I was still unqualified to apply for admission to UW. However, after reading numerous self-awareness books, I was beginning to believe that I could not only set goals, but that I could achieve them. Instead of giving up on my desire, as I previously might have done, I visited the admissions office of a nearby community college and learned what additional classes were needed. By doing so, I created momentum.

At the community college I learned that my remaining military benefits would pay most of the tuition, and I could attend classes at night. What had been a major hurdle only days before was no longer so daunting. Time passed, as it always does, and after completing two semesters at community college, I was accepted to UW.

During my first day attending classes at the UW, I was nervous and self-conscious. However, I eventually settled into the routine and earned a spot on the Dean's List for academic achievement. While attending college, I worked part-time and lived frugally. In less than two years, I graduated with a Bachelor of Arts Degree in Political Science.

The biggest obstacle to achieving my goal had been my own scarcity thinking--beliefs which had been implanted in my mind when I was young and defenseless. I now understand that I had to replace my negative inner dialogue with positive self-talk and bigger thinking. That is exactly what I did. When I caught myself thinking thoughts of scarcity, I halted the chatter and thought the opposite. Positive thinking soon became automatic. Now, when I hear others sharing their fears and doubts, I cringe because I know that I was once "that" person. I know "that" person has been programmed to believe in scarcity, and unless they become aware of their programming, they will continue to get the same results they have always gotten.

By the time I neared graduation, I had read dozens of books about goal setting, spirituality, inspiration, and the law of attraction. I was a believer, and was convinced that I could hold any image in my mind's eye, and the vision would eventually manifest into reality. I decided to begin the next phase of my life in a better climate, so I committed to moving to Santa Barbara, California. When I told friends of my plans, they usually responded by saying, "Santa Barbara is too expensive. You won't be able to afford to live there. " However, I knew that once I had chosen my new goal, and held the vision in my mind's eye as if I was already living in Santa Barbara, that Source would conspire with me to create a new reality. I should mention that I had never been to Santa Barbara. I knew nobody there, and had no job waiting for me. My only plan was to find a place to live in exchange for working around the home. I had no doubt that things would work out.

During the last week of May 1997, I began driving south on Interstate 5. Besides my old truck, all I possessed was a new bachelor's degree, $400 cash, and a dream. I arrived in Santa Barbara on a Monday afternoon and checked into a motel just outside of town. Fortunately, I located a Sunday newspaper in a waste basket. This find was important as the Internet was in its infancy, and I had no computer or access to the Internet. In the Sunday classified ads, I came upon an ad that read, "Responsible male wanted to share home with elderly woman."I immediately called and agreed to meet for an interview. The person I met was the caretaker of an elderly woman who lived alone, in an ocean view home, in the hills above Santa Barbara. The homeowner did not feel safe living alone, and she wanted a roommate to stay overnight, in exchange for free rent. I moved in two days later. I had moved to one of the most beautiful and expensive cities in the world, and had found ocean view accommodations--rent free. This move was an example of stepping off a cliff and knowing that a step would appear.

In the same Sunder paper I had circled an ad which read, "DJ wanted – will train."I called the number, and explained that I had just moved to Santa Barbara, and was in need of employment. I was hired as a wedding DJ. Several days later, I was appearing at weddings in an around Santa Barbara, playing music and learning the wedding business. Within two years, I was earning $50 hourly for part-time employment.

If I had listened to my peers in Seattle, I never would have embarked on my journey to sunny California. Or, I would have waited several years for the conditions to be perfect before I dared pursue my dream. I went after what I wanted instead of accepting what was offered. It was just a shift in my thinking. Instead of drifting with the current, I was charting my own course. I was steering the ship, with my mind. My inner thoughts were becoming my outer reality.

JOE ROGAN

"So instead of investing your time in a passion, you've sold your life to work for an uncaring machine that doesn't understand you. That's the problem with our society. And what's the reward? Go home and get a big TV."

Joe Rogan

Several years ago, UFC commentator, actor and comedian Joe Rogan said on his podcast, "Be the hero of your own life."This statement did not connect with me the first time I heard it. However, I listened to Rogan's podcast repeatedly until I understood the importance of his statement. Rogan was saying that instead of just setting and achieving individual goals, we can create an entirely new persona, if we choose. Until that time, I had been setting and achieving individual goals using the law of attraction, but I had not given much thought about the entire person I wanted to become.

I took Rogan's words to heart and created a new image in my mind's eye. I envisioned myself as competent, kind, thoughtful, funny, capable, and confident. I saw myself as a sailor, and a pilot, surrounded by caring friends, in a variety of beautiful locations around the world. I saw myself as financially free, living a life of purpose, fun and adventure. I crowded out my lingering self-doubt and replaced scarcity thoughts with positive images of the entire person I imagined I could be. I began seeing myself as the hero of my own life as Rogan had unknowingly challenged me to become. I faked confidence until I felt it. After all, others appear confident because that is the image they project to the world. Why shouldn't it be the same for you and me?

It was during this time that I decided I could become an airline pilot even though I was in my late 40s. I continued listening to podcasts featuring motivational and inspirational speakers. I wrote out my new desire, and a selected a date that the goal would be accomplished. I visualized myself in a pilot uniform in the flight deck of a large commercial jet airplane. I even declared to my wife and others that I was going to become an airline pilot. My wife believed me, but others could only see me for what I was doing at the time. At that time in my life, I was effectively a paper pusher for the government. Since most people cannot see themselves fulfilling their dreams, they certainly could not visualize me giving up a secure job with a pension to attempt something that seemed impossible to them. In fact, a few colleagues laughed when I told them I would be leaving my desk job to fly passenger jets. Instead of support, people freely shared their negative views, as if their fears and doubts should apply to me, as well as them. This is why it can be dangerous to share your dreams. Many of your friends, family, and coworkers will not encourage and support you. They are not intentionally being cruel, but are simply responding according to their scarcity belief system. After all, my coworkers were mostly paper pushers too. Surely, none of them had dreamed of spending their lives sitting in a cubicle, shuffling papers. Getting outside one's comfort zone is unlikely to happen for most people, so it is best to only share your goals with likeminded dreamers.

Undeterred by the dream killers, I drove to the airport where I had worked as a flight instructor nearly 13 years earlier and inquired into additional training. Coincidentally, two airline pilots were there to recruit new pilots to their company. I guess it was my lucky day! Or, was Source putting the right people in my path? Still, I had much work to do. I studied and trained for hundreds of hours, and during June 2014, I passed the written exam for my Airline Transport Pilot license with a score of 98%. I kept in contact with the airline recruiters, and by 2015 I had accumulated 1,500 flight hours. I was 48 years old and was ready to apply to an airline.

After submitting my application, I received an offer to interview with one of the largest airlines in the United States. The airline flew me to Denver for an interview, and I was offered a job that same day. I should point out that during the prior decade, I had only flown a tiny Cessna airplane for pleasure; I only flew in good weather and rarely at night. The only similarity between the Cessna I had been flying and the jet aircraft I would be learning to fly was that both aircraft had wings.

When I was hired by the airline, I had been the least experienced applicant and probably the oldest person in my training class. Several of the other more experienced pilots failed to complete the rigorous training and were dismissed. Nevertheless, after a few months, I had achieved my goal. I became an airline pilot at age 49! Today, at age 50, I have been certified to fly an even bigger jet, valued at $35,000,000.

I share my story only to convince you that you can create the life you deserve and desire. Once we understand and accept this truth, our lives will begin to change. My life of frustration and unhappiness began to change after I understood that my inner belief system had kept me imprisoned inside my comfort zone. My life has since become an amazing journey, and the journey gets more exciting each year. After all, I am sitting at my computer, literally writing the next chapter of my life.

HOW IT HAPPENED

"You need a plan to build a house. To build a life, it is even more important to have a plan or goal."

Zig Ziglar

Looking back on the past two decades, I realize that none of what I accomplished was overly difficult. It was simply a matter of choosing a goal and a due date, writing the goal on paper, keeping it visible, visualizing the outcome, and feeling the emotion as if the goal had already been achieved.

It is important to note that I did not manifest my desires by sitting on the sofa. I had to study and report for work or attend class. However, I was going to show up and work somewhere doing something. Why not do work that is enjoyable? When we feel passionate about our goals, it doesn't feel like work. If we are not passionate about our work, we can either change how we feel about our work or change the work we do. If you are not where you want to be in this moment, take comfort in the knowledge that you will be there soon. Try your best to enjoy your current job or situation and be grateful that it allowed you to know what you want, by knowing what you don't want. If I had never changed jobs, I would still be bagging groceries. Anyway, you don't want a job; you want a career. You want to spend your time doing something that adds value to your life and the lives of others. There are millions of career opportunities in the world and millions more will be available tomorrow.

Don't be ruled by fear. Know that you create your life with your mind, and you are not here on earth to be miserable. You are here to enjoy the ride! We are the creators of our lives. Your neighbor is not creating your life. Your parents are not creating it. And politicians are not creating it either. Eliminate the parts of your life that bring pain instead of pleasure. Listen to your emotions.

HAVE I IMPROVED MY LIFE?

"You have the power to heal your life, and you need to know that. We think so often that we are helpless, but we're not. We always have the power of our minds…Claim and consciously use your power."

Louise Hay

By adding a rudder to my life, I graduated from a university, found a loving partner, invested in real estate in expensive, southern California, bought an ocean view home on a private golf course, earned and saved a respectable amount of money, fulfilled my desire of becoming an airline pilot, and learned to sail. I travel extensively, maintain a high level of health and fitness, and I am usually happy and fulfilled. I didn't accomplish more in my life because I worked harder. I accomplished more because I thought differently.

PART VIII

THE LAW OF ATTRACTION WORKS

*"Through our eyes, the universe is perceiving itself.
Through our ears, the universe is listening to its
harmonies. We are the witnesses through which the
universe becomes conscious of its glory, of its
magnificence."*

Alan Watts

Any doubts I may have had about the power of
Source and the law of attraction melted away after
becoming an airline pilot. By harnessing the
power of my subconscious mind, my non-physical
thought manifested into physical reality. That is
literally what happened. I have been consumed
with self-improvement for more than two decades.

This topic is what keeps me up at night. It is my passion. I have decided to make self awareness my life's work--my next career. I will publish this book and embark on a speaking tour to include podcast, radio, television, and other appearances. I will not rest until one of my books becomes a best seller, and I become a successful speaker. After all, others have done what I am attempting and all things must be possible in an infinite universe. The law of attraction always works. Good or bad, it always works. It is a law, much like the law of gravity.

A SUGGESTION

"If you are ready for the secret, you already possess one half of it. Therefore, you will readily recognize the other half the moment it reaches your mind."

Napoleon Hill

We must first know what brings us pleasure before we commit to a desire. If creating art is your passion, but you fear you cannot pay your bills as an artist, I agree with you. If you focus on failure and poverty, you will manifest failure and poverty. If you write down your goal to become an artist and begin visualizing yourself as a successful artist, your goal will manifest into physical reality. If art is truly your passion, you will never feel like you're working. Source will assemble your non-physical thought into physical reality, and you will become the artist you imagine. Source will not judge. Both Source and gravity respond predictably. Gravity operates the same whether you are pushing a boulder up a mountain or rolling the same boulder down a mountain. Gravity can make our lives difficult or make our lives easier. Source responds similarly. It reacts predictably regardless if your beliefs are true or untrue.

You and I and everything are manifestations of Source. Source beats our hearts, heals our wounds, creates planets, and supports life. Once you accept this truth and use the law of attraction to your benefit, your life will change forever. There will be no going back. It costs you nothing. You don't have to show up anywhere or convert anybody. You just have to harness the power of your mind to create the life you desire. It's not too good to be true. It's true. I am staking my reputation on it.

IMAGINATION

"The number one reason people fail in life is because they listen to their friends, family, and neighbors."

Napoleon Hill

Most of us don't dream big enough. Our minds hold us back because we lack confidence or imagination. What was once thought impossible by prior generations is now considered normal. Just imagine the improvements that have occurred in your lifetime. Life moves fast. When I was a kid, it was impossible to remove the telephone from my house because it was tethered to the wall. Our family car required petroleum. I had to go to the library to look up information. Our only television received four channels; the signal came through the air and was caught by an antenna. While all these conveniences are now considered outdated, at the time they were just normal. That was the way things were. We did not imagine a car running on batteries, television signals coming from space, phones becoming mobile computers, and we did not envision the Internet. However, somebody else did imagine these inventions. Think back two centuries when most humans could not imagine that powered flight was possible. Humans have always had the ability to fly, even to the moon and beyond. We only lacked the belief that it was possible. The earth hasn't changed. Only our belief in what is possible changed. Once Oroville and Wilbur believed they could build a machine that could fly, they created the technology to make flight possible. Their belief created a new reality. Only 66 years later, humans walked on the surface of the moon. The Wright brothers thought big, but somebody else thought even bigger when they imagined spacecraft traveling beyond our solar system. What do *you* believe is possible?

PART IX

CONCLUSION

"We can only receive what our minds are capable of accepting."

Robert Anthony

In the beginning of this book, I wrote that I could explain in one or two pages how you can create the life you have imagined, but I cautioned that you might not believe me because you might consider my suggestions too simple. Now do you believe? To summarize, decide what it is that you desire. Be specific, but don't fret about the details. If you want a new car, see the car in your mind. Visualize the color, the smell, and the feel of the seats. Imagine yourself driving in your neighborhood. Visualize the car parked in your garage, or in your assigned space. Print a picture of the desired car and tape it to your bathroom mirror. Keep a copy in your wallet and another on your desk. Do not keep a photo in your current car; that is rude. Appreciate your current car and be grateful for its service. Think about how soon you want your new car. Don't expect the car by the end of the day, as you're not a magician. Be confident that your car is coming to you. You do not have to know how. Source will handle the details. Your subconscious mind is the conduit to Source and your message has been relayed. Source has figured out how to create everything in the universe, so manifesting your car won't be a problem. The only problem will be your doubt and hesitation. Be patient like a farmer planting corn. Corn stalks don't emerge from the soil the following day. Corn grows on its own schedule. It knows when the time is right. The conditions must be welcoming. Corn requires the right season, the right soil, and the right amount of water. Babies are like that too. You can't expect a baby to emerge the day after your honeymoon, unless you are already pregnant. Babies arrive right on schedule.

The schedule for creation already exists. You cannot rush it. Be patient and enjoy life in the meantime.

If you desire more money, the same principles apply. I suggest you begin by telling yourself that you welcome any and all money into your life. Wealth can take any form. Don't paint yourself into a corner and tell your subconscious that you want $500,000 in gold bars to fall out of an armored truck during your drive to work. Be open to inheriting a home, or a business, or a car collection. Be open to winning the lottery. Expect checks to be delivered that you were not expecting. Expect to earn more from your current employment. Personally, I always carry at least $500 cash in my wallet. I do this because I once saw a reporter ask Warren Buffet, one of the richest men in America, how much cash he had in his wallet. Buffet had $500, so that's how much cash I carry. If I had zero cash in my wallet, I might feel poor, so I do my best to feel rich. I often relax in the lobbies of beautiful hotels and imagine I'm a guest there. I walk in the best neighborhoods, select my favorite houses, and see the home as my own, regardless of the cost. I imagine my bank statement showing $3,000,000 in my savings account. I am not consumed with money but I welcome it and money flows to me.

I previously wrote about getting the body you desire. However, let's discuss this topic some more. First, be kind to yourself. Next, visualize the body you want to have. See yourself in the swimsuit you want to wear this summer. Imagine how you will feel in your new body; visualize where you are and what you're wearing. If you hold the image in your mind and know that Source is working for you, not against you, the image in your mind will become your reality. You will begin eating better and exercising more. Get advice from people who already have the body you want. When I go to the gym, I often imitate the guy with the best body. He already figured it out so I don't have to reinvent the wheel. Don't get advice form a person who is always on a diet. Seek advice from the person who already has the body you desire. They won't be offended. I would not get investment advice from a broke neighbor or relationship advice from a therapist who has been divorced five times. Help is available everywhere if you look. Skip the fad diets, as they are a waste of your time and effort. No matter what the commercials say, the only thing that matters is calories ingested versus calories burned. It is not a mystery; it is science. If having a certain look is important for you, you will make time for exercise and you will stop buying potatoes chips and start buying vegetables. Also, whatever food you have in your house is the food you will eat. So don't go shopping while hungry or you'll end up with a shopping cart full of unhealthy food. If you put unhealthy food in your cart, you will have unhealthy food in your pantry, and you will eat it.

If you want more happiness, start thinking happier thoughts. Recall memories that made you laugh and even plan your next vacation, even if it's a year away. I always like to have something fun and exciting to anticipate. Be grateful for your health, your friends, your family, your job, and your home. We have it pretty good where I live. Even the poor among us have televisions, cars, and an Internet connection. Do not trust that money will bring you happiness. Happiness is an emotion. Listen to your emotions. Emotions are clues sent by your subconscious mind, reminding you what is important. If you feel happy at the beach then go to the beach more often. If you feel sad in your dingy apartment, visualize a new apartment. Envision a home where you really want to live. Go after what you want, not what you think you can get.

We know happiness because we know sadness. Don't get too down on yourself when sadness appears. Let it happen and know it will pass. Sadness reminds us of the beauty of happiness. Happiness should be our top goal. After all, many of us wrongly believe that the new car, new career, new lover, and new apartment will bring the happiness we seek. But we can go straight to happiness. I was happy when I was broke and beginning my new life in California. I am always finding time to do the things that bring me happiness. Sometimes it's a walk, sometimes it's a movie, sometimes it's time spent with my wife, sometimes it's time spent with a cat on my lap. I feel happy in so many different ways.

Too many people believe their past will determine their future. This is untrue. Our thoughts determine our future. Think about what you want. Imagine the income you desire. Imagine the person you want to be. Be the hero of your life. Think about how your heroes act; then act like them. See yourself at age 90, looking back at your life. Are you proud of the life you have lived? Did you make a difference? Did life happen to you or did you happen to life? Happiness is not hiding in hard work, a bottle, or a container of ice cream. Happiness is found by living the live you imagine for yourself. Happiness is yours for the taking. This moment is all we ever have. The clock is ticking. It is your life to live. If not now, when?

I truly hope that you have enjoyed reading my first book. When you see positive changes in your life I want you to write me at vegetarianpilot@gmail.com and share your story, so I can share it with others in future books. I am grateful for you and I hope we meet someday soon. A better life can be yours!

About The Author

ROBERT LAWRENCE is an airline pilot, sailor, adventurer, and an author. He served in the US Army 3/75th Ranger Regiment from 1985-86 and is a graduate of the University of Washington in Seattle. He currently lives in Southern California with his wife and two rescue cats.

Made in the USA
Las Vegas, NV
25 November 2022

60241857R10069